MW01055724

Literature Circle Guide:

A Wrinkle in Time

by Tara McCarthy

SCHOLASTIC
PROFESSIONAL BOOKS

New York • Toronto • London • Auckland • Sydney
• Mexico City • New Delhi • Hong Kong • Buenos Aires

Guide written by Tara McCarthy
Edited by Sarah Glasscock
Cover design by Niloufar Safavieh
Interior design by Grafica, Inc.
Interior illustrations by Mona Mark

Credits: Cover: Jacket cover from A WRINKLE IN TIME by Madeleine L'Engle. Copyright © 1962 by Madeleine L'Engle. Used by permission of Random House Children's Books, a division of Random House, Inc. Interior: Author photo on page 9 copyright © 1992 by Sigrid Estrada. Used with permission.

ISBN: 0-439-27169-X

Contents

To the Teacher

As a teacher, you naturally want to instill in your students the habits of confident, critical, independent, and lifelong readers. You hope that even when students are not in school they will seek out books on their own, think about and question what they are reading, and share those ideas with friends. An excellent way to further this goal is by using literature circles in your classroom.

In a literature circle, students select a book to read as a group. They think and write about it on their own in a literature response journal and then discuss it together. Both journals and discussions enable students to respond to a book and develop their insights into it. They also learn to identify themes and issues, analyze vocabulary, recognize writing techniques, and share ideas with each other—all of which are necessary to meet state and national standards.

This guide provides the support materials for using literature circles with *A Wrinkle in Time* by Madeleine L'Engle. The reading strategies, discussion questions, projects, and enrichment readings will also support a whole class reading of this text or can be given to enhance the experience of an individual student reading the book as part of a reading workshop.

Literature Circles

A literature circle consists of several students (usually three to five) who agree to read a book together and share their observations, questions, and interpretations. Groups may be organized by reading level or choice of book. Often these groups read more than one book together since, as students become more comfortable talking with one another, their observations and insights deepen.

When planning to use literature circles in your classroom, it can be helpful to do the following:

✸ Recommend four or five books from which students can choose. These books might be grouped by theme, genre, or author.

✸ Allow three or four weeks for students to read each book. Each of Scholastic's *Literature Circle Guides* has the same number of sections as well as enrichment activities and projects. Even if students are reading different books in the *Literature Circle Guide* series, they can be scheduled to finish at the same time.

✸ Create a daily routine so students can focus on journal writing and discussions.

✸ Decide whether students will be reading books in class or for homework. If students do all their reading for homework, then allot class time for sharing journals and discussions. You can also alternate silent reading and writing days in the classroom with discussion groups.

Read More About Literature Circles

Getting the Most from Literature Groups by Penny Strube (Scholastic Professional Books, 1996)

Literature Circles by Harvey Daniels (Stenhouse Publishers, 1994)

Using the *Literature Circle Guides* in Your Classroom

Each guide contains the following sections:

❋ background information about the author and book

❋ enrichment readings relevant to the book

❋ Literature Response Journal reproducibles

❋ Group Discussion reproducibles

❋ Individual and group projects

❋ Literature Discussion Evaluation Sheet

Background Information and Enrichment Readings

The background information about the author and the book and the enrichment readings are designed to offer information that will enhance students' understanding of the book. You may choose to assign and discuss these sections before, during, or after the reading of the book. Because each enrichment concludes with questions that invite students to connect it to the book, you can use this section to inspire them to think and record their thoughts in the literature response journal.

Literature Response Journal Reproducibles

Although these reproducibles are designed for individual students, they should also be used to stimulate and support discussions in literature circles. Each page begins with a reading strategy and follows with several journal topics. At the bottom of the page, students select a type of response (prediction, question, observation, or connection) for free-choice writing in their response journals.

◆ Reading Strategies
Since the goal of the literature circle is to empower lifelong readers, a different reading strategy is introduced in each section. Not only does the reading strategy allow students to understand this particular book better, it also instills a habit of mind that will continue to be useful when they read other books. A question from the Literature Response Journal and the Group Discussion pages is always tied to the reading strategy.

If everyone in class is reading the same book, you may present the reading strategy as a mini-lesson to the entire class. For literature circles, however, the group of students can read over and discuss the strategy together at the start of class and then experiment with the strategy as they read silently for the rest of the period. You may want to allow time at the end of class so the group can talk about what they noticed as they read. As an alternative, the literature circle can review the reading strategy for the next section after they have completed their discussion. That night, students can try out the reading strategy as they read on their own so they will be ready for the next day's literature circle discussion.

◆ Literature Response Journal Topics
A literature response journal allows a reader to "converse" with a book. Students write questions, point out things they notice about the story, recall personal experiences, and make connections to other texts in their journals. In other words, they are using writing to explore what they think about the book. See page 7 for tips on how to help students set up their literature response journals.

1. The questions for the literature response journals have no right or wrong answers but are designed to help students look beneath the surface of the plot and develop a richer connection to the story and its characters.

2. Students can write in their literature response journals as soon as they have finished a reading assignment. Again, you may choose to have students do this for homework or make time during class.

3. The literature response journals are an excellent tool for students to use in their literature circles. They can highlight ideas and thoughts in their journals that they want to share with the group.

4. When you evaluate students' journals, consider whether they have completed all the assignments and have responded in depth and thoughtfully. You may want to check each day to make sure students are keeping up with the assignments. You can read and respond to the journals at a halfway point (after five entries) and again at the end. Some teachers suggest that students pick out their five best entries for a grade.

Group Discussion Reproducibles

These reproducibles are designed for use in literature circles. Each page begins with a series of discussion questions for the group to consider. A mini-lesson on an aspect of the writer's craft follows the discussion questions. See page 8 for tips on how to model good discussions for students.

◆ **Literature Discussion Questions:** In a literature discussion, students experience a book from different points of view. Each reader brings her or his own unique observations, questions, and associations to the text. When students share their different reading experiences, they often come to a wider and deeper understanding than they would have reached on their own.

The discussion is not an exercise in finding the right answers nor is it a debate. Its goal is to explore the many possible meanings of a book. Be sure to allow enough time for these conversations to move beyond easy answers— try to schedule 25–35 minutes for each one. In addition, there are important guidelines to ensure that everyone's voice is heard.

1. Let students know that participation in the literature discussion is an important part of their grade. You may choose to watch one discussion and grade it. (You can use the Literature Discussion Evaluation Sheet on page 33.)

2. Encourage students to evaluate their own performance in discussions using the Literature Discussion Evaluation Sheet. They can assess not only their own level of involvement but also how the group itself has functioned.

3. Help students learn how to talk to one another effectively. After a discussion, help them process what worked and what didn't. Videotape discussions if possible, and then evaluate them together. Let one literature circle watch another and provide feedback to it.

4. It can be helpful to have a facilitator for each discussion. The facilitator can keep students from interrupting each other, help the conversation get back on track when it digresses, and encourage shyer members to contribute. At the end of each discussion, the facilitator can summarize everyone's contributions and suggest areas for improvement.

5. Designate other roles for group members. For instance, a recorder can take notes and/or list questions for further discussion. A summarizer can open each literature circle meeting by summarizing the chapter(s) the group has just read. Encourage students to rotate these roles, as well as that of the facilitator.

◆ **The Writer's Craft:** This section encourages students to look at the writer's most important tool—words. It points out new vocabulary, writing techniques, and uses of language. One or two questions invite students to think more deeply about the book and writing in general. These questions can either become part of the literature circle discussion or be written about in students' journals.

Literature Discussion Evaluation Sheet

Both you and your students will benefit from completing these evaluation sheets. You can use them to assess students' performance, and as mentioned above, students can evaluate their own individual performances, as well as their group's performance. The Literature Discussion Evaluation Sheet appears on page 33.

Setting Up Literature Response Journals

Although some students may already keep literature response journals, others may not know how to begin. To discourage students from merely writing elaborate plot summaries and to encourage them to use their journals in a meaningful way, help them focus their responses around the following elements: predictions, observations, questions, and connections.

Have students take time after each assigned section to think about and record their responses in their journals. Sample responses appear below.

◆ **Predictions:** Before students read the book, have them study the cover and the jacket copy. Ask if anyone has read any other books by Madeleine L'Engle. To begin their literature response journals, tell students to jot down their impressions about the book. As they read, students will continue to make predictions about what a character might do or how the plot might turn. After finishing the book, students can re-assess their initial predictions. Good readers understand that they must constantly activate prior knowledge before, during, and after they read. They adjust their expectations and predictions; a book that is completely predictable is not likely to capture anyone's interest. A student about to read *A Wrinkle in Time* for the first time might predict the following:

I know this book is science fiction, so I predict it's going to take place in the future or on some other planet. But the three kids in the cover look pretty average and so does the land below them. The science fiction part is the strange bird-human. Who are those little old ladies down on the ground? The artist wouldn't put them there unless they were important characters in the story.

◆ **Observations:** This activity takes place immediately after reading begins. In a literature response journal, the reader recalls fresh impressions about the characters, setting, and events. Most readers mention details that stand out for them even if they are not sure what their importance is. For example, a reader might list phrases that describe how a character looks or the feeling a setting evokes. Many readers note certain words, phrases, or passages in a book. Others note the style of an author's writing or the voice in which the story is told. A student just starting to read *A Wrinkle In Time* might write the following:

At the beginning of the story, the atmosphere is sort of scary, with a storm brewing and Meg feeling all alone. Then when Meg goes down to the kitchen and talks with her mother and brother, the atmosphere feels cozy and warm. I can see that Meg gets a lot of comfort from her family.

◆ **Questions:** Point out that good readers don't necessarily understand everything they read. To clarify their uncertainty, they ask questions. Encourage students to identify passages that confuse or trouble them and emphasize that they shouldn't take anything for granted. Share the following student example:

Who exactly is this woman called Mrs. Whatsit? How come she stole sheets? Why is Mrs. Murry so startled by the word tesseract?

◆ **Connections:** Remind students that one story often leads to another. When one friend tells a story, the other friend is often inspired to tell one, too. The same thing often happens when someone reads a book. A character reminds the reader of a relative, or a situation is similar to something that happened to him or her. Sometimes a book makes a reader recall other books or movies. These connections can be helpful in revealing some of the deeper meanings or patterns of a book. The following is an example of a student connection:

Meg seems to feel (and to be) different from most other kids. She feels inferior in some ways. She reminds me a lot of Mafatu in Call It Courage *because Mafatu also felt left out, weak, and different.*

The Good Discussion

In a good literature discussion, students are always learning from one another. They listen to one another and respond to what their peers have to say. They share their ideas, questions, and observations. Everyone feels comfortable about talking, and no one interrupts or puts down what anyone else says. Students leave a good literature discussion with a new understanding of the book—and sometimes with new questions about it. They almost always feel more engaged by what they have read.

◆ **Modeling a Good Discussion:** In this era of combative and confessional TV talk shows, students often don't have any idea of what it means to talk productively and creatively together. You can help them have a better idea of what a good literature discussion is if you let them experience one. Select a thought-provoking short story or poem for students to read, and then choose a small group to model a discussion of the work for the class.

Explain to participating students that the objective of the discussion is to explore the text thoroughly and learn from one another. Emphasize that it takes time to learn how to have a good discussion, and that the first discussion may not achieve everything they hope it will. Duplicate a copy of the Literature Discussion Evaluation Sheet for each student. Go over the helpful and unhelpful contributions shown on the Literature Discussion Evaluation Sheet. Instruct students to fill it out as they watch the model discussion. Then have the group of students hold its discussion while the rest of the class observes. Try not to interrupt or control the discussion and remind the student audience not to participate. It's okay if the discussion falters, as this is a learning experience.

Allow 15–20 minutes for the discussion. When it is finished, ask each student in the group to reflect out loud about what worked and what didn't. Then have the students who observed share their impressions. What kinds of comments were helpful? How could the group have talked to each other more productively?

You may want to let another group experiment with a discussion so students can try out what they learned from the first one.

◆ **Assessing Discussions:** The following tips will help students monitor how well their group is functioning:

1. One person should keep track of all behaviors by each group member, both helpful and unhelpful, during the discussion.

2. At the end of the discussion, each individual should think about how he or she did. How many helpful and unhelpful checks did he or she receive?

3. The group should look at the Literature Discussion Evaluation Sheet and assess their performance as a whole. Were most of the behaviors helpful? Were any behaviors unhelpful? How could the group improve?

In good discussions, you will often hear students say the following:

"I was wondering if anyone knew . . ."

"I see what you are saying. That reminds me of something that happened earlier in the book."

"What do you think?"

"Did anyone notice on page 57 that . . ."

"I disagree with you because . . ."

"I agree with you because . . ."

"This reminds me so much of when . . ."

"Do you think this could mean . . ."

"I'm not sure I understand what you're saying. Could you explain it a little more to me?"

"That reminds me of what you were saying yesterday about . . ."

"I just don't understand this."

"I love the part that says . . ."

"Here, let me read this paragraph. It's an example of what I'm talking about."

About *A Wrinkle in Time*

A Wrinkle in Time has become a classic, but it almost didn't get published. Madeleine L'Engle's manuscript was rejected by more than twenty publishers who thought the story was too complex for young readers. After being published, the book was called "anti-Christian" by some religious groups and "too Christian" by some reviewers.

A Wrinkle in Time is a part of L'Engle's Time Quartet. The other books in the series are *A Wind in the Door*, *A Swiftly Turning Planet*, and *Many Waters*. In 1963, *A Wrinkle in Time* was awarded the Newbery Medal.

To research the science she incorporates into her books, L'Engle questions friends who are scientists. She also reads about subjects such as particle physics and quantum mechanics. About the word *tesseract*, L'Engle says, "I came across the word . . . in a science article and got kind of fascinated by it."

About the Author: Madeleine L'Engle

Madeleine L'Engle was born in New York City in 1918. Her mother Madeleine Hall Barnett Camp was a pianist, and her father Charles Wadsworth Camp was a writer. When L'Engle was a child, musicians and people from the theater frequently visited the Camps' house.

At the age of twelve, Madeleine and her family moved to Europe. She attended school in Switzerland and then South Carolina. After graduating from Smith College in 1941, L'Engle moved to New York. She wanted to be a playwright so she joined a theater company. Then L'Engle met and married the actor Hugh Franklin. They moved to Connecticut and ran a general store. Of that time, L'Engle writes, "I must admit that participating in the life of a small but active community, running a large farmhouse, and raising three children were the perfect ways 'not' to write a book. But I did manage to write at night. I have written since I could hold a pencil, . . . and writing for me is an essential function, like sleeping and breathing."

Ten years later, Madeleine L'Engle and her family moved back to New York City. In addition to children's books, she has written adult novels, essays, poetry, and plays.

Other Books by Madeleine L'Engle

An Acceptable Time

And Both Were Young

The Arm of the Starfish

Camilla

Dragons in the Water

A House Like a Lotus

Many Waters

Meet the Austins

Moon by Night

A Ring of Endless Light

A Swiftly Tilting Planet

Troubling a Star

A Wind in the Door

Young Unicorns

Enrichment:
The Nature of Science Fiction

Writers of science fiction understand important theories in physics, keep up with technological developments and goals, and have some well-founded ideas about where science might lead us next. They pose complex questions for their readers to consider, such as, "What's the difference between a robot and a human being?" or "How would we humans react to an intelligent being who was different from us in many ways?" As you read *A Wrinkle in Time*, you'll find yourself not only grappling with the scientific meaning of time and space but also thinking about the nature of courage, the battle between good and evil, and the role that religion may play in our lives.

Science fiction writers face the same challenges that all writers do. They have to create sympathetic, believable characters and plots that keep the readers turning pages. In the nineteenth century, the writers H.G. Wells and Jules Verne wrote extremely popular books about the thrills of space travel while raising important questions about the possible abuses of technology to create destructive civilizations. Aldous Huxley, in *Brave New World*, and George Orwell, in *1984*, tell intriguing stories about everyday life in "perfect" worlds; their books show that a perfect society would put severe limits on individuals' rights to express themselves.

A Wrinkle in Time is one of the very first sci-fi novels to be written especially for young people. It has paved the way for hundreds of other science fiction books for young readers that deal with big issues, such as the need to protect the natural environment (H.M. Hoover's *Only Child*), the responsibilities that come with being intelligent (Robert O'Brien's *Mrs. Frisby and the Rats of NIMH*), and the difficulty of finding your own place and role in a new community (Anne McCaffrey's *Dragonslinger*).

If you were going to write science fiction, which big issue or idea would you choose? Why is that issue important to you? Try your hand at writing a science fiction story. You can even make your family the main characters!

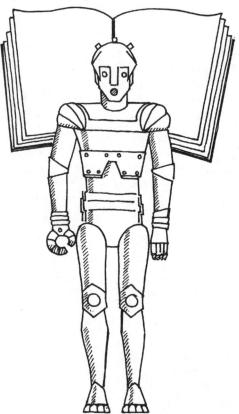

Enrichment: Guardian Spirits

In William Shakespeare's play *Macbeth*, the hero is stumbling about on a foggy moor when he meets three witches named the Weird Sisters. Although the women are gruesome looking, they try to help Macbeth by warning him of what might happen if he's not careful. Unfortunately, Macbeth ignores the advice of these three guardian spirits.

Almost every culture in the world contains folklore about such supernatural beings. Living invisibly in the world, guardian spirits became visible to humans and active in their lives only in times of great need. For example, Aeolus, the spirit of the wind in Greek mythology, answered the prayers of sailors who needed strong winds to carry them to their destinations. Arifa, a kindly spirit in the old folk beliefs of Morocco, stepped in to protect families–especially infants–when danger threatened. Often, these guardian spirits not only protect but also teach, guide, and advise.

A common characteristic of guardian spirits is that they have the ability to change shape. They may appear as humans, animals, or ghostly presences. Sometimes they're gloriously beautiful; sometimes they're tremendously ugly. Sometimes they're mischievous; sometimes they're serious. Because of a guardian spirit's appearance, it's often up to the human being involved to decide whether the spirit— whatever its shape—has come to offer help or do harm.

In modern times, we tend to think that believing in guardian spirits is out-of-date. Yet guardian spirits live on in many stories we've enjoyed and traditions we celebrate. Think about Tinkerbell in *Peter Pan*. How would the Lost Boys ever have escaped from the pirates without her help? Children today still love stories about the Tooth Fairy and the Sandman.

In *A Wrinkle in Time*, you'll meet three guardian spirits who have most of the characteristics discussed above. Be alert to the emergencies in which the spirits intervene, the shapes they take, and the roles they play in helping the human protagonists achieve their goals. Why do you think humans first created stories of guardian spirits? Why do these stories continue to be popular today? Think about what your own responses might be to meeting someone—or something—like Mrs. Whatsit, Mrs. Who, or Mrs. Which.

MACBETH

Enrichment: Family Stories

Although *A Wrinkle in Time* is science fiction and fantasy, it's also a family story. The overarching aim of Meg Murry, the heroine, is to rescue her father from the grip of the evil IT and then safely return to the warmth and love of their home. Meg's adventure is something like Dorothy's in *The Wizard of Oz*, for Dorothy also gets carried off to an unearthly place and begins the long struggle to return to her home.

In some family stories, the family is traditional—mother, father, and children are in one place. Examples include most of Laura Ingalls Wilder's *Little House* books and Carol Ryrie Brink's *Caddie Woodlawn*. More common, perhaps, are the family stories in which someone is missing, as in *A Wrinkle in Time*, either for a long period or permanently. In *Little Women*, the four March sisters and their mother make daily life as cheerful as they can while their father is away. In Alice Dalgliesh's *The Courage of Sarah Noble*, Sarah must stay alone in a wilderness cabin she's built with her father while he goes back to get the rest of the family. Even with family members missing, the main characters or protagonists in these stories are sustained by the values and affection they share with their parents and siblings.

In real life, family life is sometimes tough, and this reality is often reflected in literature. In her semi-autobiographical book *Journey to Topaz*, Yoshiko Uchida shows the hardships endured by Japanese-American families who were held in prison camps in the United States during World War II. In *Roll of Thunder, Hear My Cry*, Mildred Taylor tells about an African American family's struggle to hold onto their land during the Great Depression.

In real life, some families are constructed by people who have lost—forever or temporarily—their own families. Fiction reflects this, too. For example, in Patricia MacLachlan's *Sarah, Plain and Tall*, frontier children whose mother has died think they have found a new mother in Sarah. Then they have to face the possibility that she, too, may leave them.

As you read *A Wrinkle in Time*, think about what kind of family story it is. How is the Murry family like a traditional family? Is it possible for a family in a work of science fiction to be traditional? Are the Murrys facing any real life problems? Is there any place in the book where one of the characters is taken care of by someone else in a loving and caring way?

Name _____ Date _____

A Wrinkle in Time
Before Reading the Book

Reading Strategy:
Discovering What You Already Know

Take some time to think about the title of this book. Study the cover illustration. What other books have you read that broke the boundaries of time? What movies or television shows have you seen that deal with that subject? Spend five minutes writing about the aspects of time-travel that most intrigue you. Write as fast as you can. Don't edit yourself along the way.

Writing in Your Literature Response Journal

A. Write about one of these topics in your journal. Circle the topic you chose.

1. What do you already know about the author Madeleine L'Engle and the books she has written? What do you know about science fiction?

2. What qualities or personal characteristics would a person have to have to take part in a voyage that would overcome the boundaries of time?

3. Who's the bravest person you've ever met? Describe him or her. In what way is he or she different from ordinary people? What special gifts or talents does that person have?

4. Write about an event in your life when you felt truly powerful. Contrast this with an occasion when you felt powerless and helpless.

B. What were your predictions, questions, observations, and connections about the book? Write about one of them in your journal. Check the response you chose.

❑ Prediction   ❑ Question   ❑ Observation   ❑ Connection

Literature Circle Guide for *A Wrinkle in Time* • Scholastic Professional Books

Name _____ **Date** _____

A Wrinkle in Time
Before Reading the Book

For Your Discussion Group

❋ If you've read any other books by
Madeleine L'Engle, discuss what major
themes or ideas she is concerned with.

❋ *A Wrinkle in Time* is unusual because it
deals not only with science-fiction
events but also with everyday events.
Make a two-column chart that contrasts
how a science-fiction story and a
realistic story might deal with the
following situations:

the mysterious disappearance of
someone the hero or heroine loves

the problems the hero or heroine faces
as he or she seeks the missing person

the characters the heroine or hero meets along the way

❋ Discuss the following issues:

Is a heroic person someone who feels no fear, or someone who does something daring
in spite of fear? Why do you say so?

When a hero or heroine needs help, to whom might he or she turn? Do such choices
always turn out to be wise? Give some examples from books you've read.

In situations where you've felt you were in danger, what special sayings, memories,
beliefs, or goals encouraged you to behave bravely and wisely?

❋ When you've finished discussing these questions and issues, take some time to write
in your journal about the meaning of heroism. Include a sentence or two that tells
whether your idea of heroism has changed as a result of your group discussion.

Literature Circle Guide for *A Wrinkle in Time* • Scholastic Professional Books

Name _____ Date _____

A Wrinkle in Time
Chapter 1

Reading Strategy: Visualizing

Madeleine L'Engle begins the story by presenting the setting
and the main character, Meg (Margaret Murry). The opening
sentence—"It was a dark and stormy night"—is a kind of inside joke with writers
because it's an old, overused opening line for establishing a setting that's ghostly or
mysterious. L'Engle then goes on to show Meg in action, so you get to visualize this
main character and get to know her. As you read the first four pages, copy a few
sentences or phrases that help build a setting that's mysterious and threatening.

Writing in Your Literature Response Journal

A. Write about one of these topics in your journal. Circle the topic you chose.

   1. In Chapter 1, L'Engle helps you visualize the main character, Meg, by describing
   her, including what Meg thinks and feels, what she does, and how she does it.
   Use this data to write your own description of Meg. Accompany your written
   description with a drawing of her in one of the scenes in the chapter.

   2. In this chapter, Meg remembers that her father said the following about
   Charles Wallace:

   *There's nothing the matter with his mind. He just does things in his own way
   and in his own time.*

   Do you feel that most people are encouraged to do things in their own way and in
   their own time? Is it always better to do everything your way—no matter what
   the situation is? Give examples to support your thinking.

**B. What were your predictions, questions, observations, and connections as you
read? Write about one of them in your journal. Check the response you chose.**

   ❏ Prediction   ❏ Question   ❏ Observation   ❏ Connection

Name _____ **Date** _____

A Wrinkle in Time
Chapter 1

For Your Discussion Group

✳ This first chapter introduces several characters
  in addition to Meg. From the actions and
  words of these characters or from details
  provided by the author, you've probably
  formed mental pictures or visualized what
  these characters look like. Exchange ideas about the appearance of the following
  characters: Charles Wallace, Sandy and Dennys, Mrs. Murry, Fortinbras, and
  Mrs. Whatsit.

✳ Although he never appears in this chapter, Meg's father is obviously an important
  character and an object of concern. What are your guesses about what's happened to
  him? What do you think a tesseract is?

✳ Here comes strange Mrs. Whatsit, bouncing into what seems like a normal
  household—except for Charles Wallace and a missing father. What are your predictions
  about how Mrs. Whatsit will change the family's life?

Writer's Craft: Synonyms

Writers are always precise about the language they use. Instead of writing about a big
egg, an author might use the following **synonyms**, or words that have the same or
almost the same meaning: *huge, enormous, gigantic*. Think about a big egg, and then
visualize a huge egg. You probably visualized two very different kinds of eggs.

The characters in this book don't hesitate to use precise language, either. Find the following bits of dialogue in the chapter. Use your own knowledge, the sentence context,
and a dictionary to write a synonym for each underlined word.

> *"You're much too <u>straightforward</u> . . ."*
> *". . . I want to be <u>exclusive</u> about her . . ."*
> *"My, but isn't he <u>cunning</u>."*
> *"<u>Prodigious</u>," Mrs. Murry said.*

Literature Circle Guide for *A Wrinkle in Time* • Scholastic Professional Books

Name _____   **Date** _____

A Wrinkle in Time
Chapters 2–3

Reading Strategy:
Making Inferences

To infer is to independently draw a conclusion based on facts the writer gives you. Good writers don't always tell their readers everything. Instead, they supply the facts that will enable the readers to make inferences. For instance, from the facts that L'Engle supplies, what can you infer about Meg's problems at school?

Writing in Your Literature Response Journal

A. **Write about one of these topics in your journal. Circle the topic you chose.**

1. Which details in the story lead you to infer that Mrs. Who and Mrs. Whatsit are not ordinary human beings?

2. Meg says she accepts that Charles Wallace is different but that she doesn't understand it. What's the difference between accepting something and understanding it?

3. Meg's mother seems to be involved in a project that she can't yet fully share with her children. From the facts that L'Engle gives, what do you infer about Mrs. Murry's project?

B. **What were your predictions, questions, observations, and connections as you read? Write about one of them in your journal. Check the response you chose.**

❑ Prediction   ❑ Question   ❑ Observation   ❑ Connection

Literature Circle Guide for *A Wrinkle in Time* • Scholastic Professional Books

Name _____ Date _____

A Wrinkle in Time
Chapters 2–3

For Your Discussion Group

✳ Charles Wallace and Calvin recognize that they're both sports. The word *sports* seems to have a special meaning here. What can you infer about the meaning of *sports* from its context?

✳ Calvin and Charles Wallace agree that Mrs. Murry is "not one of us," and that Meg is "not really one thing or the other." Discuss what the boys mean by these remarks.

✳ By the end of Chapter 3, you have some information about Meg's father, the work he did, and the circumstances of his disappearance. (Note: Cape Canaveral is now called Cape Kennedy.) Predict what may have happened to him. Explain which details in the story you based your predictions on.

Writer's Craft: Dialogue

Dialogue is the conversation within quotation marks that gives the exact words a character says. Well-written dialogue moves the plot along and reveals something important about the character who's speaking. In the following example, we learn that Meg is a math whiz:

> *Again Meg's pencil was busy. "All you have to remember is that every ordinary fraction can be converted into an infinite periodic decimal fraction. See? So 3/7 is 0.428571."*

Share with your group some dialogue in these chapters that adds to your understanding of the concerns, strengths, or interests of characters in the story.

Literature Circle Guide for *A Wrinkle in Time* • Scholastic Professional Books

Name _____ Date _____

A Wrinkle in Time
Chapter 4

Reading Strategy: Point of View

Point of view refers to the person who tells the story. In the first-person point of view, the story is told in the first person (*I* did this, *I* saw that, and so on). A story can also be told from the third-person point of view, as in *A Wrinkle in Time*. We see events mostly the way Meg experiences them, and she's referred to in the third person (*She* did this, *She* saw that, and so on). Think about how the story would change if it were told from the third-person point of view of another character, such as Mrs. Murry or Mrs. Whatsit.

Writing in Your Literature Response Journal

A. **Write about one of these topics in your journal. Circle the topic you chose.**

1. Choose an event from Chapter 4. Use your imagination to rewrite it from the point of view of Charles Wallace. Use words like *he, his,* and *Charles* to focus on Charles Wallace's experience of the event.

2. The chapter opens with a vivid description of what Meg experiences as she's "wrinkled" from Earth to Uriel. Write in your own words what she senses.

3. In your opinion, what is the most amazing, attention-grabbing thing about Uriel? How is this sci-fi land different from other places you've read about? If you were Meg, could you be happy living on Uriel forever? Explain your reasons.

B. **What were your predictions, questions, observations, and connections as you read? Write about one of them in your journal. Check the response you chose.**

❏ Prediction   ❏ Question   ❏ Observation   ❏ Connection

Literature Circle Guide for *A Wrinkle in Time* • Scholastic Professional Books

Name _____   **Date** _____

A Wrinkle in Time
Chapter 4

For Your Discussion Group

✳ The differences between the speech patterns of Mrs. Whatsit, Mrs. Who, and Mrs. Which are becoming more and more obvious. The different patterns reveal something about the ages, history, and nature of these mysterious beings. Explore the following questions with your group:

Why is Mrs. Whatsit the best of the three at communicating with Meg, Charles Wallace, and Calvin? What might being the youngest have to do with it?

Mrs. Who peppers her speech with quotations from Greek, Latin, French, and other languages. Assuming that she's not just showing off, why do you think she does this?

Mrs. Which is the oldest of the three and, apparently, the leader. She drags her words out, almost as if speech is a long-forgotten skill. What are some possible explanations for this?

Writer's Craft: Description

As Meg rides on the back of the transformed Mrs. Whatsit, she's amazed by the changing scenes around her. To help readers visualize the experience from Meg's point of view, L'Engle describes the landscape vividly. In addition, she uses words and phrases, such as *around*, *through*, *upward*, and *over*, to help readers imagine exactly where things are, as in the following sentence:

> *Below them there were still rocks; above them the rocks continued to reach up into the sky. . . .*

Although L'Engle's descriptions help readers see the planet Uriel, each reader's vision will be different. The writer supplies the descriptive words and phrases, but the reader supplies the details by using the power of her or his imagination. If each member of your group drew a picture of Uriel, each picture would be quite different. Try it and see!

Literature Circle Guide for *A Wrinkle in Time* • Scholastic Professional Books

Name _____ Date _____

A Wrinkle in Time
Chapters 5–6

Reading Strategy: Making Predictions

You've probably been paying careful attention to the plot of this story. So much is happening! In addition to keeping track of what's going on, you're also probably making predictions about what's going to happen next. Like all good writers, Madeleine L'Engle encourages her readers to make predictions by dropping hints about what the future holds for the characters. Based upon your reading of these chapters, write down a prediction. List the facts and clues in the story that you used.

Writing in Your Literature Response Journal

A. Write about one of these topics in your journal. Circle the topic you chose.

1. Before she leaves, Mrs. Whatsit gives different objects to Meg, Charles Wallace, and Calvin. Mrs. Who gives her glasses to Meg, along with instructions about when to use them. From the nature of these gifts, what problems do you predict these three characters might encounter?

2. The residents of Camazotz behave like robots. Predict what will eventually be revealed about these people.

3. You probably know the saying, "One picture is worth a thousand words." What do the pictures in Chapter 5 help you understand?

B. What were your predictions, questions, observations, and connections as you read? Write about one of them in your journal. Check the response you chose.

❏ Prediction   ❏ Question   ❏ Observation   ❏ Connection

Literature Circle Guide for *A Wrinkle in Time* • Scholastic Professional Books

Name _____ **Date** _____

A Wrinkle in Time
Chapters 5–6

For Your Discussion Group

✶ Something called IT is closely related to CENTRAL Central Intelligence. Put this fact together with other information about Camazotz. Predict and discuss what IT might be.

✶ A battle with the Dark Thing has been raging through the universe for centuries. Use the details supplied in these chapters to predict what the Dark Thing is. Start by discussing the qualities of the people who have battled the Dark Thing in the past.

✶ L'Engle adds humor now and then to this serious story. One form the humor takes is puns, or word play. Discuss the meanings of the following words and phrases and how L'Engle uses them to make puns:

witch: a magical, powerful person
Camelot: an imaginary kingdom where goodness reigns
Fuller Brush man: a vendor who sold household products door-to-door
happy medium: a good compromise between extremes

Writer's Craft: Character Development

In a well-written story, the reader discovers more and more about each character as the story moves along and the characters meet new challenges. A good writer doesn't explain everything about a character at the beginning of a story. For example, in Chapters 5 and 6, we're beginning to see Calvin as someone who's very cautious and somewhat skeptical. We're starting to see an impatient streak in Meg when she insists on hurrying to find her father. The most significant development is in the character of Charles Wallace. At the beginning of the story, he seems to be a child with unusual powers of perception. He is also a real buddy to his sister Meg. In these chapters, Charles seems to be separating from Meg and to have plans of his own. With your group, find clues in the story that show Charles Wallace is even more different from ordinary people than you first thought he was. Share your predictions about how he'll behave in the future.

Literature Circle Guide for *A Wrinkle in Time* • Scholastic Professional Books

Name _____   Date _____

A Wrinkle in Time
Chapters 7–8

Reading Strategy:
Summarizing

The plot thickens! Before you proceed
with your reading, it can help to
summarize what's happened so far in
this fast-paced story. When you
summarize, you state in a few
sentences the major events of the
story. To summarize, you can rely on your memory or you can look back at the chapters
you've read to zero in on key events. Summarizing will help you better understand what
will happen next. After reading Chapters 7 and 8, summarize them.

Writing in Your Literature Response Journal

A. **Write about one of these topics in your journal. Circle the topic you chose.**

1. In one hundred words or less, summarize why Meg, Charles Wallace, and Calvin
are on Camazotz.

2. Charles Wallace says that the food delivered to them tastes like sand, while Meg
says it tastes like a great turkey dinner. Why do they have different opinions
about how the food tastes?

3. In his changed form, Charles Wallace says that nobody is unhappy on Camazotz.
Meg replies, "Maybe if you aren't unhappy sometimes, you don't know how to
be happy." What does Meg mean? Do you agree or disagree with her? Explain
your reasons.

B. **What were your predictions, questions, observations, and connections as you
read? Write about one of them in your journal. Check the response you chose.**

❏ Prediction   ❏ Question   ❏ Observation   ❏ Connection

Literature Circle Guide for *A Wrinkle in Time* • Scholastic Professional Books

Name _____   Date _____

A Wrinkle in Time
Chapters 7–8

For Your Discussion Group

✳ The man with red eyes and Charles Wallace describe Camazotz as a perfect society because people there are freed from making decisions. They have given control of their lives to a higher authority. What seems to be the cost of giving in? Discuss whether a perfect society could ever be created *without* people giving in to a higher authority.

✳ These chapters focus on the changes Charles Wallace undergoes. Discuss why the man with red eyes is particularly interested in having Charles Wallace on his side.

✳ The "new" Charles Wallace tells Meg that her differences have caused problems for her at school. Discuss how Meg is different. What kinds of differences cause problems for students in your school? When can being different be positive? How might Meg's differences turn out to be assets as she seeks to rescue her father?

Writer's Craft: Atmosphere

In literature, **atmosphere** is the feeling and mood created by the writer's use of description. For example, L'Engle creates an atmosphere of dread and worry as she describes the entrance hall of the CENTRAL Central Intelligence building.

> *Marble benches lined three of the walls. People were sitting there like statues. The green of the marble reflecting on their faces made them look bilious.*

All those sliding doors! All those people waiting like robots! All those automatic, robot-like responses to questions! With your group, rewrite a description of the entrance hall to change the atmosphere. Make the hall seem like a friendly and safe place where someone could get his or her problems solved quickly.

Literature Circle Guide for *A Wrinkle in Time* • Scholastic Professional Books

Name _____ **Date** _____

A Wrinkle in Time
Chapter 9

Reading Strategy: Asking Questions

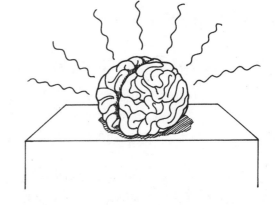

As you intensely follow the developments in an exciting story, you're bound to ask questions. Why can't Meg's father see? Why is Charles Wallace so quick to fall prey to the man with red eyes? Why have Mrs. Whatsit, Mrs. Which, and Mrs. Who left Meg on her own? In fact, if a story didn't make questions like these pop into your mind, it would be a very dull story indeed! What keeps you reading is your search for the answers. List some of the questions you have about the story so far.

Writing in Your Literature Response Journal

A. **Write about one of these topics in your journal. Circle the topic you chose.**

1. Write some questions you would like to ask the characters at this point in the story. For example, you might ask Calvin, "Why did you ever volunteer to go on this trip?" You might ask Mr. Murry, "How did you get sealed up in that box?"

2. Imagine you're visiting Camazotz. Write some questions you'd ask yourself as you traveled around the community.

3. At this point in the story, Meg has mixed feelings about Charles Wallace. Describe these feelings and explain why Meg has them.

B. **What were your predictions, questions, observations, and connections as you read? Write about one of them in your journal. Check the response you chose.**

❏ Prediction   ❏ Question   ❏ Observation   ❏ Connection

Literature Circle Guide for *A Wrinkle in Time* • Scholastic Professional Books

Name _____ **Date** _____

A Wrinkle in Time
Chapter 9

For Your Discussion Group

✳ To counteract the power of the man with red eyes and IT, it seems useful to shout out things like nursery rhymes and the periodic table of elements. Discuss why repeating them seems to protect one—at least temporarily—from the evil on Camazotz.

✳ Meg says, "*Like* and *equal* are not the same thing at all!" Discuss what she might mean by this statement. Do you agree or disagree with her? Tell why.

✳ The people on Camazotz—if that's what they are!—seem to have no individual memories. What are the advantages of remembering one's own history? What are the disadvantages?

Writer's Craft: Conflict

In literature, **conflict** refers to the struggle between characters or outside forces (**external conflict**) or between opposing ideas and feelings in a character's mind (**internal conflict**). Skillful writers set up exciting conflicts so readers will want to find out how these conflicts will be resolved. An external conflict in *A Wrinkle in Time* is between Meg and IT. An internal conflict is Meg's struggle to figure out how to behave toward the changed Charles Wallace. With your group, look through the chapters you've read and identify other external and internal conflicts.

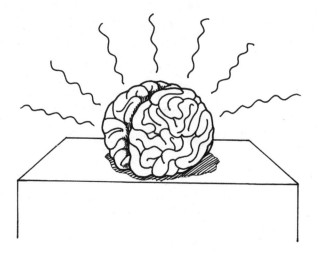

Literature Circle Guide for *A Wrinkle in Time* • Scholastic Professional Books

Name _____ Date _____

A Wrinkle in Time
Chapters 10–11

Reading Strategy:
Drawing Conclusions

You draw conclusions as you read. You
put together information the writer gives
you to reach ideas on your own. For
example, from reading about Meg's
reaction to her father's inability to rescue
Charles Wallace, you can draw the
conclusion that she thinks her father is
pretty wimpy. Keep in mind, though, that
your conclusions may change based on what happens next in the story. Think about
some of the conclusions you've made as you read this story.

Writing in Your Literature Response Journal

A. Write about one of these topics in your journal. Circle the topic you chose.

1. Carefully reread Mr. Murry's conversations with Meg. What is your conclusion
about what he's really afraid of?

2. Meg is much slower to recover from her trip from Camazotz to Ixchel than Calvin
and Mr. Murry are. Why do you think this is so? What might be slowing down
her recovery?

3. The beings on Ixchel seem kind and helpful. Do you trust them? Explain why or
why not.

B. What were your predictions, questions, observations, and connections as you
read? Write about one of them in your journal. Check the response you chose.

❐ Prediction   ❐ Question   ❐ Observation   ❐ Connection

Literature Circle Guide for *A Wrinkle in Time* • Scholastic Professional Books

Name _____ Date _____

A Wrinkle in Time
Chapters 10–11

For Your Discussion Group

✳ What is the nature of the experiment Mr. Murry was involved in? How did it go wrong?

✳ Update your understanding of tessering based on what you've learned to far from this story. What exactly is tessering? How is it different from going back in time or forward in time? In your opinion, is tessering a realistic goal for the immediate future? For us Earthlings, what might be the value of tessering?

✳ In these chapters, Meg seems ill and homesick but also angry and determined. Discuss what she may find out about herself as the story moves toward a conclusion.

Writer's Craft: Imagery

Imagery is language that appeals to the senses. Writers use imagery to help readers experience what the characters are seeing and feeling. The following excerpt appeals to our senses of touch and sight:

> *As though Meg were a baby, Aunt Beast bathed and dressed her, and this new garment, though it was made of a pale fur, was lighter than the lightest summer clothes on earth. Aunt Beast put one tentacled arm about Meg's waist and led her through long, dim corridors in which she could see only shadows, and shadows of shadows, . . .*

With your group, find other examples of imagery in *A Wrinkle in Time.* Read the examples aloud to one another. Discuss what senses the excerpts appeal to.

Name _____   Date _____

A Wrinkle in Time
Chapter 12

Reading Strategy: Rereading

In a story with as many twists and turns
as this one has, you may want to reread
parts of chapters to better understand
how and why things turn out as they do.
For example, you may want to reread to
find out why Mrs. Murry didn't want the
children to know exactly what their
father was involved in. Rereading can also help you understand how Meg's rebellious,
defiant attitude at school served her well in rescuing Charles Wallace. Studying a story
by rereading it can also help you as a writer: You'll see how writers plant clues along the
way that make the endings believable. What have you learned about writing by
rereading parts of *A Wrinkle in Time*?

Writing in Your Literature Response Journal

A. **Write about one of these topics in your journal. Circle the topic you chose.**

1. Reread the first chapters to find out what Meg hated about herself. Then write
about how Meg's incredible adventure may help her value herself.

2. Reread the parts of Chapter 6 that tell about the objects that Meg, Charles Wallace,
and Calvin were given. Write about how these characters used the objects to
escape the evil on Camazotz.

3. Meg comes to realize that she's the only one who can rescue Charles Wallace.
Why does she feel this way?

B. **What were your predictions, questions, observations, and connections as you
read? Write about one of them in your journal. Check the response you chose.**

❏ Prediction   ❏ Question   ❏ Observation   ❏ Connection

Literature Circle Guide for *A Wrinkle in Time* • Scholastic Professional Books

Name _____   Date _____

A Wrinkle in Time
Chapter 12

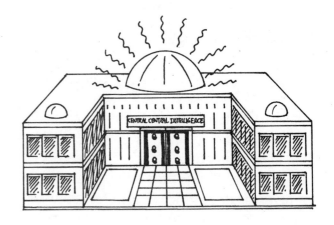

For Your Discussion Group

✳ In a complex story like this one, even rereading may not answer all your questions. For example, it's never spelled out in the book exactly what the Black Thing is. You do get some hints about the Black Thing through its commanding presence on Camazotz. Discuss what this Black Thing might be and why it's so horrifying. How would the Black Thing change your life if it took charge of Earth?

✳ Mrs. Who quotes the Bible to show that weak or foolish people can overcome evil. Discuss how this applies to Meg, Calvin, and Charles. How are they weak and foolish? What foolishness enables Meg to overcome evil?

✳ Mrs. Whatsit uses the rules of the sonnet form to explain how a person can be free yet law-abiding. Reread the part of Chapter 12 in which Mrs. Whatsit explains the form of a sonnet. With your group, write a sonnet that summarizes *A Wrinkle in Time*.

Writer's Craft: Theme

A book's **theme** conveys important ideas about life. The writer doesn't usually state the theme directly. It's up to readers to discover the theme for themselves. Each reader may discover a different theme in a story. For example, the following sentence is a theme in *A Wrinkle in Time*: Through perseverance and courage, you can realize your goal. With your group, discuss and record other themes that you find in this story.

Literature Circle Guide for *A Wrinkle in Time* • Scholastic Professional Books

Name _____ **Date** _____

A Wrinkle in Time
After Reading

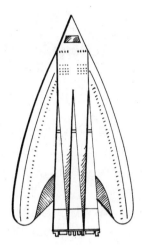

Every good story, whether it's science fiction or realistic fiction or biography, contains the following: interesting characters, a problem to solve, challenges to overcome and decisions to make, and a solution to the problem.

✱ Review and summarize the components as they appear in *A Wrinkle in Time* by answering the questions below. Record your work in your journal, and then discuss your ideas in your literature circle.

   1. Who is the most interesting character in this book? Why does that character interest you the most?
   2. What problem does this character face?
   3. What challenges does the character have to overcome to solve the problem?
   4. What decision does the character make?
   5. How does the character finally solve the problem?

✱ Good stories, whatever their main genre, usually incorporate aspects of other genres. For example, there's an element of mystery in *A Wrinkle in Time* as Meg and her companions seek to solve her father's disappearance. Make a chart like the one below to help you identify the different genres in the book. Go through *A Wrinkle in Time*, and complete your chart.

Science Fiction	Religion & Philosophy	Humor	Realistic Fiction

✱ Share your chart with your group. Discuss the similarities and differences in your charts.

Literature Circle Guide for *A Wrinkle in Time* • Scholastic Professional Books

Individual Projects

1. Through tessering, an adventurer overcomes the amount of time necessary to travel vast distances in space. Another aspect of time often explored in science fiction is the possibility of going backward in time to experience events that happened long ago, or forward in time to experience event that haven't happened yet. Read sci-fi stories that deal with time travel. Report on these stories to your group.

2. Write a travel guide for people who want to take the same trip that Meg did. Include do's, don'ts, sights along the way, and suggested items to take. Illustrate and bind your travel guide.

3. Choose three or four scenes from *A Wrinkle in Time* that contrast in atmosphere—for example, atmospheres of comfort, threat, and wonder. Illustrate the scenes and write captions for them.

Group Projects

1. *A Wrinkle in Time* was published in 1962. Since then, there have been great gains in the exploration of space. Have members of your group investigate independently and make detailed notes about different aspects of space travel. When individual research is complete, share and discuss your findings. As a group, research space travel from 1962 to the present. Present your findings in a timeline.

2. Develop a readers' theater presentation of *A Wrinkle in Time*. Start by going through each chapter to identify key problems and conflicts. Translate these into written dialogue between the characters, much of which you can pick up from the book itself. Make copies of the script for each actor, and practice at least once before presenting it to your class.

3. Writers of science fiction often create new words to describe the people, places, and events in their work. Remember the word *tesseract* in this book? Work with your group to invent your own science-fiction vocabulary. Include proper and common nouns, verbs, adverbs, and adjectives. Use a dictionary format to write definitions of your new words.